W9-CAH-117

A ROOKIE READER

ONE WHOLE DOUGHNUT,

ONE DOUGHNUT HOLE

By Valjean McLenighan

Illustrations by Steven Roger Cole

Prepared under the direction of Robert Hillerich, Ph.D.

870927

CHILDRENS PRESS ™

CHICAGO

Library of Congress Cataloging in Publication Data

McLenighan, Valjean.
    One whole doughnut, one doughnut hole.

    (A Rookie reader)
    Summary: Text and illustrations introduce
homophones, words that sound the same but have
different meanings and often, different
spellings.
        1. English language — Homonyms — Juvenile
    literature. [1. English language — Homonyms]
I. Cole, Steven Roger, ill. II. Title. III. Series.
PE1595.M38 1982   428.1   82-12838
ISBN 0-516-02031-5

One WHOLE doughnut.

One doughnut HOLE.

3

A PIECE.

A PEAR.

6

A PAIR of pears.

8

My AUNT.

An ANT on my aunt.

9

10 Sack of FLOUR.

Sack with FLOWER.

11

SO?

So, SEW!

13

Big TOE.

Big toe in TOW.

A PANE.

A pane in PAIN. Ow!

18   I SEE.

I see the SEA.

RIGHT turn.

WRITE, "turn."

Lift a WEIGHT.

WAIT for a lift.

One sweet SCENT.

24

One-CENT sweet.

25

All HERE?

Can't HEAR.

28 Pay a FARE.

Play FAIR!

29

Off TO school.
Take me, TOO.
30 Goodbye, you TWO!

WORD
LIST

a	goodbye	pane	taxi
all	hear	pay	the
an	here	peace	this
ant	hole	pear	to
aunt	I	piece	toe
big	in	play	too
candy	is	right	tow
can't	lift	sack	turn
cent	me	scent	two
doughnut	my	school	you
elevator	of	sea	wait
fair	off	see	weight
fare	on	sew	whole
flour	one	shop	with
flower	ow	so	write
for	pain	sweet	
	pair	take	

About the Author

Valjean McLenighan, a graduate of Knox College in Galesburg, Illinois, became interested in writing children's books during her stint as an editor at a large midwestern publishing company. Since that time, many of her children's books have been published.

Though she nearly always has a book project in the works, Valjean finds time for a variety of other interests including the theater, children's television, and travel. She lives on the North Side of Chicago and enjoys spending time with her many friends in the Midwest and around the world.

About the Artist

With this book, **Steven Roger Cole** makes his first "solo flight" as an illustrator. He was formally educated to be a fine artist and art teacher, while he informally became a singer-entertainer, actor, cartoonist, and commercial artist. He has for many years been a professional portrait artist, and has recently added caricatures to his repertoire. As an actor, Mr. Cole has a flair for comedy; as a cartoonist, he strives to be funny on paper; and as a human being, he is occasionally very amusing. He has a fine arts degree from the University of Michigan, a teacher's certificate from Eastern Michigan University, a natural rapport with children, a collection of 78 rpm records, lots of ideas, size 14 shoes, no nickname, and growing confidei ce for the road ahead.